A WINTER TOUR
THROUGH
INDIA, BURMAH
AND
STRAITS

A WINTER TOUR
THROUGH
INDIA, BURMAH
AND
STRAITS

GYAN

Published by

Gyan Publishing House
5, Ansari Road
Daryaganj, New Delhi-110002
Phone: 011-47034999, 9811692060
E-mail: books@gyanbooks.com

Distribution Network
gyanbooks.com
India, USA, Canada, UK, Australia

ISBN: 978-93-7097-167-7 (PB)
First Published, 1880

2nd Impression 2025

Printed at: Gyan Press, Delhi.

A WINTER TOUR THROUGH INDIA, BURMAH AND STRAITS
Arthur H. E. FALK

A WINTER TOUR

THROUGH

INDIA, BURMAH

AND

THE STRAITS

BY

H. E. FALK

LONDON
LONGMANS & CO., PATERNOSTER ROW.
1880.

PREFACE.

DURING long voyages in tropical latitudes, time does occasionally hang heavy upon your hands, although the itinerant voyager in search of health and rest cannot choose a more delightful mode to attain his object. An hour per diem set apart for writing, to record observations and note striking events of your progress, fills a physical and mental void admirably.

Many kind friends, both in India and in Europe, have induced me to make public property what was but intended for a few eyes. The burning question of the day is the policy by which the greatest gem of this globe, and the most magnificent jewel in the British crown, is to be directed. Most crude, most mystical notions pervade the popular conception of this great country, and the unfortunate hypercritical style adopted always by the unofficial and official Anglo-Indian does not tend to lift the veil.

If my little book, which does not claim either perfect accuracy or erudite exhaustion of the subjects, with which it deals, will give the reader the reflection of the bright and pleasant days I have spent during the past winter, my object will be gained. I do claim for my notes a perfectly unbiassed conception and honest relation of my observations. An active merchant of upwards of forty years' standing in the great port of Liverpool, I am not accustomed to book-making—or the experienced rhetoric and phraseology of book-making; I must on this plea crave the kindly consideration of my readers and critics.

H. E. FALK.

CATSCLOUGH, CHESHIRE,

April, 1880.

A WINTER TOUR 1879-80

THROUGH

INDIA, BURMAH AND THE STRAITS.

A WINTER TOUR 1879-80

THROUGH

INDIA, BURMAH AND THE STRAITS.

IT is October, 1879.

The Clerk of the Weather at Washington has prophesied a severe winter again. Why, therefore, stop among the fogs and icicles? Away to regions which don't know them!

It was said: and ladies pull their summer gear from dusty drawers; gentlemen look up tropical clothing; passages are taken by the "Cunarder" for Malta, from Liverpool direct, and the grey skies of Old England are left behind. We are scudding down channel our moderate 11 knots on the 31st October. Three days bring us into bright blue: the "Bay" you barely touch in your course from Liverpool; hence the passage is preferable to that from Southampton, as your comfort on board is not broken into by this proverbially stormy sea. Finisterre, St. Vincent, grand old "Gib.," Cape Bone, &c., &c., are left behind, and on the ninth day we cast anchor in Malta harbour. The cheerful, bright, and clean island smiles its welcome, and after having duly settled the ladies in respectable "Dunsford Hotel" for the winter, to await our return, we take passage by one of the numerous daily sailers for Alexandria, to spend a week in Egypt *en route.*

A word about Egypt *en passant.* We were here five years ago: to our view a great transformation for the better has taken place, and the bondholders' millions, we think, have been, if not judiciously, at all events well spent for the purpose of beautifying the cities and facilitating the internal traffic and comfort of the country, which must eventually bear fruit. We think the old Khedive badly used, and to talk of the "poverty," "bankruptcy," and other euphonious cant of Egypt is, to our notion, rank rubbish. The "poor" fellaheen is a jolly bright specimen of the sons of toil, and in comparison with our agricultural labourer would bear a scrutiny without fear. I am sure an unbiassed, intelligent observer would award him the palm of the better lot: no wrinkles in his brow, no pinching care in his eye, and clearly no anxiety for "house," "coal," and "blanket," as none are wanted in these climes. The ride through the rail-netted Delta of the Nile is most instructive and pleasing to the agricultural mind: such soil, such crops, can only be seen in semi-tropical and tropical regions. Two crops annually — wheat and cotton one year, sugar and beans the next — and so on in endless succession since the days of the Pharoahs. Thus has this wonderful soil proved its self-sustaining and recuperative powers: there seems, to our view, no need for improvement by implements or artificial fertilizers. The plough to-day is the same which was held by the peon in the days of Moses, the ox is the same, the fellah the same; they have not changed, and they need not change for the well-being of the country; the bountiful soil and the bountiful sun are there, and will produce as much as man requires and calls for. If you don't ask him for anything more than he requires for his own frugal needs, he will lie basking in the shade of his village palm, and, with true philosophy, exclaim, "Why should I produce what I don't need?" but tax him, as a natural sequence to the inexorable logic of improvement of the state, and he will have no difficulty in producing as much as you ask for, in reason. His political friends will, of course, exclaim "Tyranny," but, I opine, such exclamations will be taken *quantum valeant.*

CAIRO

is a delightfully cheerful place to stay at for a few days, weeks or months. Everything has been done by the late ruler to make it an attractive resort for strangers. The gardens, the style of architecture of the new streets, the bridges, the avenues, the roads—all are made with a view to the comfort of European refinement. The old town and bazaars have huge attractions, the latter for ladies especially; the ancient monuments, pyramids, sacred spots and trees, (*inter alia* a mythical fig-tree under whose foliage the Virgin and Joseph are said to have rested) for the archæologists and the curious. Under any circumstances a few days on the road to India are well, agreeably and profitably spent there.

We join the P. and O. mail at *Suez*—a spot which is unfortunate enough to leave few friends behind. It is hot, dirty and dull beyond description. Therefore the half-day or whole day which you are compelled to spend there, awaiting the passage of your steamer through the "desert ditch," you must count as a blank in your existence.

A rasping northerly breeze bowls us down the Gulf of Suez, and having installed ourselves in our cabin — the home of the next fortnight — we begin to take stock of the company on board. The steamer is crowded: 130 passengers in the first class, 40 ladies, 10 children, and their necessary belongings — the chief prevailing element, of course, civil and military officers of the Indian Government, a dozen generals, colonels, and captains, some judges, some doctors, and some representatives of great mercantile houses in Bombay, Calcutta, and Madras. The whole in the course of a few days begin to amalgamate, and pleasant days and evenings are spent, as is usual when people are bound to make themselves agreeable, on penalty of being expelled from society. The enquiring mind has great opportunities on these trips, and we hear wonderful stories from north, south, east and west of India, of sporting adventures, travels in high altitudes, sketches of native and European character in jungle, court and station life. Well, the time passes; the northerly breeze, which carried us down the Red Sea for two days in grand style, suddenly lulls, and eventually turns dead ahead, due south; the thermometer, which had been kept down by the norther to moderate 82°-85° in the shade, creeps up to 90°-92°, and along with it a depressing atmosphere begins to silence the merry hum of the ship. These 48 hours in the latitudes of the teens in the Red Sea are always the most trying; they are the rainless regions of the earth,—not a green blade or leaf is to be seen, although we have often most picturesque groups of rocks on islands or mainland in view. The wind blows as through a hot blast tube, and you are fairly melting. In Aden it rains only once every three years, and there is an apocryphal story of a place in Egypt, near the second cataract, where no rain has been known for 70 years. Meantime the water below is as pure azure as the canopy of heaven above, not a vestige of cloud, and at night the stars sparkling, as they only know how in these regions. There is something supremely elevating and ethereal in these heaven-lit nights, and you must go to the East to see it, for the Western tropics don't give you an equal chance.

ADEN

is reached. Six hours for change of mails, cargo, and coaling are more than the passenger requires, as it is a most uninteresting place. And now we set our course for Bombay direct, seven days more, through one of the most charming seas of the world—the Indian Ocean. It is hot—85°-90°—but the air feels crisp and cheery—no depression with the heat. Balls and concerts are the order of the night daily, and the time glides on so pleasantly that the general phrase of regret becomes: "How sorry we shall be when to-morrow we have to part." The fact is, these trips in the large passenger steamers are the most pleasant pic-nics you can have; the ordinary idea associated with our rough northerly waters finds no place in them, the ship glides along, as on a lake, and *mal de mer* is quite unknown. Impatient minds would like to go a little faster, and have less of the leisurely style, which characterizes all eastern motions, and I must confess, for the credit of British enterprise, the trip to Bombay—under 6,000 miles across Europe—ought to be done in 14, instead of 18 days, as now. It would pay the P. & O. well to make proper arrangements for a swifter train service across Europe, and swifter boats from Brindisi to Alexandria and Suez to Bombay, at all events during the winter season. Crowds of passengers, who are deterred by the ancient three weeks trip, would avail themselves of a fortnight service, and who can measure the benefits which the additional light let in by ocular demonstration to the English public would produce for both England and India? How many absurd theories would vanish? How many quacks, who are now trading upon mythical hearsay, would have to pack up their wares, and hold their tongues in Indian debate? The one universal cry in India, the one great desideratum is: "British public, come and look, if you would understand India and its value to you!"

BOMBAY

is sighted; its glorious harbour lies before us; an hour, and we are landed upon "Apollo Bunder," and comfortably installed in "Watson Hotel," as the natives call it—its more extended title being "Esplanade Hotel." Now everything you see is fresh—you realize that you have entered another world. A grand, imposing town is before you; magnificent buildings, wide streets, and, above all, crowds and multitudes of the *genus homo.* This, to our view, is one of the most impressive characteristics of Asiatic life: you meet man everywhere in such masses as you cannot produce in similar circumstances elsewhere, and you feel that the cradle of the race must be within the tropics, as its most genial abode still is there. Serving spirits surround you wherever you put your foot on Indian soil; the white "Sahib" meets with deference everywhere, and we confess, the feeling of superiority, which in the first instance is thrust upon you, and but reluctantly accepted, begins to grow, until you opine at last that that traditional Assyrian story accounting for the difference of colour in mankind, viz., "White man, child of God, black man, child of Adam," may have, after all, something in it.

In Bombay you enjoy the beauty of the tropical sunset to perfection; truly the gorgeous East is mirrored in it with all its glorious surroundings of the vegetable kingdom. The picturesque Malabar Point, with the Governor's Palace and the Caves of Elephanta, are most pleasant objects for excursions. The caves are carved in the solid rock, Hindoo temples of no great merit artistically, but showing traces of sculpture, from which our later Italian artists in mediæval times have not been ashamed to borrow. They are worth a visit, if you have spare time for a day's excursion, as you are on the island introduced to the real tropical vegetation. The native town of Bombay itself contains many quaint buildings, and is abundantly ornamented by carving in wood, which has attained to great perfection in the district and still flourishes from ancient times. It is a very busy, thriving place, and a drive at sunset through the great bazaar thoroughfare, when all the mills and factories are sending forth their toilers, gives the stranger an idea of the masses which are compressed within these Indian centres of population.

After a few days' rest in Bombay we start on our journey to the North-West. A well-appointed railway, with excellent, roomy sleeping-carriages, receives you. Our first object is the holy city of Hindostan,

BENARES,

about 1,000 miles by rail from Bombay. We travel in the first instance through the Ghauts, a small mountain chain in the immediate vicinity of Bombay, and most conveniently situated for the Bombayites, who can afford the change, to get a cool temperature during the hot season. The mountains are full of picturesque points of view, and land you on the eastern side upon the real vast plain of India, which stretches from the foot of the Himalayas to the ocean, and is an almost unbroken plateau of rich alluvial soil, intersected by rivers and their tributaries, at distances which call for but very little artificial aid to make them flow where man requires to irrigate his crops.

These schemes of canalization and irrigation have called forth prodigious masses of controversy and reports, and I am inclined to lean to the side of a very intelligent native gentleman, a member of the Bengal Council, who stated to me that the old rulers of India had never lost sight of the subject, and their engineers were as clever as ours. They studied the rainfall as much, and wherever a proper locality for impounding waters existed, they used it. Nature was the best guide, and canals were but a most questionable remedy for her so-called objects, as it was found that epidemics and fevers followed the modern work of canalization, which intercepted the drainage of the country, and thus produced anything but an unmixed good. Although I approach the subject with great diffidence, as it is dealt with by such able men as Mr. Hume and Mr. Caird, I cannot help saying that their view of the fecundity of Indian soil is of the most pessimist description. Sun and water are in my opinion sufficient to recuperate any soil, else what would have become of all Europe? Manuring is but a very modern institution in farming, introduced generally almost within memory of the "oldest inhabitant." And now about the chief crops of India, rice and jute: they are grown almost entirely under water; what would be the use of manure to such? And I never heard yet of a rice-field producing a scant crop for want of anything but water!

We have reached Benares by 36 hours' travel: we have stayed two days, and seen most of its hackneyed sights, and we have had quite enough of them: 5,000 temples, mosques, and shrines, and an army of lazy, dirty priests, performing foolish, childish rites, in order to keep the unthinking multitudes in harness for their support—that is about the *summum bonum* we have from Benares. The city is fithy and mean, apart from the palatial residences of the Hindostanee rulers and princes and other very opulent Hindoos, who as a matter of religious faith have to subscribe to the irrational doctrine, that every Hindoo who wants to die happy must see Benares. However, we must not be too severe upon these religious tenets, for after all our own history shows that similar notions were prevalent amongst enlightened Christians in the middle ages, and the variety of taste which exists amongst the Hindoos as to the choice of their inferior deities finds a very opportune parallel in our own Roman ritual, which has quite as many saints of masculine and feminine gender as the Hindoo has, although the latter chooses all sorts of animal and supernatural objects for devotion, whilst the Catholic sticks to the human form divine. Both have the same faith in one Supreme God. This inferior-deity worship is kept up unquestionably by the priestly craft, who have to live by it, and who were even too strong, as events proved, for the great reformer, Buddha. He lived some five centuries B.C., and by force of his own strong will, blameless life, and powerful preaching taught the Asiatic nations a purely rational creed, with the sublime and high doctrine, "Do unto others as thou would'st be done by." So rapid was the conversion of all the Asiatic peoples that nearly the whole of the Brahministical intermediate deities were swept away. But priestcraft eventually conquered again, and, after the Bhuddistic era had run its course for a few centuries in Hindostan, the plastic, dreamy mind of the Hindoo was again brought over to the priestly rule of the Brahmins, and there we find him now. China and Japan, however, held fast to Buddha's teaching in most respects. The Brahmin faith is very harmless, and not much more vicious than a good many other schools with more civilized titles. However it sadly interferes with the progress of the people. For instance: a man becomes an outcast if he leaves India; he can't eat or drink anything that has been defiled by the touch of the unorthodox; he won't eat meat or kill any animal. Progress of Western civilization must necessarily be slow under such circumstances, unless another Buddha rises. But railways are beginning to cut at the root of the evil, and ere long these absurd superstitious rules must give way. Such is also the idea of most enlightened natives. Side by side with Hindoos live their ancient conquerors, the Mussulmans. You can recognise them at first glance by their wild eyes and more independent bearing. There is no love lost between the two neighbours, and since we bless both by equal laws and never interfere with their harmless religious amusements we have an excellent counterpoise to the ambitious plotting of either sect. The Hindoo generally recognises the beneficence of the British dominion, whilst the wild Mahomedan still casts longing eyes and hopes for a return of the magnificent past, when he rode the country like a whirlwind, and trampled the industrious dweller of the plain into the dust. The wild Tartar must always be an element of careful study and watchful anxiety to the Government, and it is for this reason and no other that the Tartar brother races must be kept away, or they might join hands and again destroy the work of a century of peace and industry, which the great Indian nation has enjoyed. The Hindoo trader and peasant wants security against this ever present danger of the ancient Mahomedan enemy, and any government whieh would be ill-advised enough to curtail the number of white troops in the country would retard the progress of industry and the advancement of the masses generally. The fashion is to call India a poor country: what grounds or reasons there are for this I have ever failed to see. A soil teeming with abundance, a climate fit for any crop, the trees exuding precious gums, the very leaves and bark yielding valuable spices, regions where the earth can be made to yield all the metals and alkalis, with the most precious building stones on the surface, and a coast indented with safe ports and rivers, stretching thousands of miles inland:—this is the poor country so-called. The fact is the reverse; it is so rich that it has always been the most coveted of possessions, and ruthless conquerors have made the people suspicious to a fault. They have pleaded always poverty to escape the exactions of the Tartar, and I am told that the bulk of the bullion which undoubtedly is poured into the country from Europe and the New World, is hoarded, buried, and converted into ornament, which can be hid away easily. To find a remedy for this great evil ought to be the problem of the clever administration of the country. I have discussed the point often, and in many distant corners of the empire, and the best remedy, on which all agree, seems to be a wide extension of railways. If you bring the means of easy and cheap communication with distant parts to the door of everybody, he avails himself of it, and the rupee which is buried will be unearthed to satisfy the love for travel, which is very strongly developed in India among the natives. Travel will educate the ignorant, it will teach him to use his opportunities, and eventually make the so-called starveling into an opulent, independent peasant. Railways can't fail to pay handsomely in India, for the element of success is multitude. Anyone traversing India and seeing the masses of travellers cannot fail but become convinced. Hitherto engineering has been very defective—needless expenditure on grand works, studious avoidance of the great centres of population, and similar errors, of which we have not been free at home; but this no doubt will be altered, and the cheap metre gauge ought to net the country by thousands of miles. Local and provincial guarantees will find the money, and natives will not be slow to take to good investments at their doors. The middle trading class of natives is both prosperous and opulent, and if you give them a chance of indulging a little in their pastime of gambling in stocks, they would sooner invest in public securities than look to the usurers' trade which they now more or less all follow. The iron industries of England should look this question up, for here is a grander and far safer field for them than the west affords. 15,000 miles of rails laid over India would solve many questions, political and social; no fear of famines in future if the produce of one province can be brought with a few hours' notice to the other; no fears of raids and mutinies if each garrison is within a few hours' reach of the other. And above all, the produce would be brought to market and obtain its legitimate value, instead of wasting and fading unused, and the hoarded rupees would be brought into circulation and exchange would resume its ancient standard. I have been told that there are many districts in the North-West and Rajpoot country where wheat is only worth 2s. a bushel and a pair of fine bullocks £1. From Benares we struck into the lovely plains of

OUDH,

on the new railway to Lucknow. It was a charming sight, the vast green wheat-fields extending hundreds of miles, which stretches on this level plain before your view. They sow their wheat and peas here as an intermediate crop during the winter in November, and reap it in March to make room for sugar, cotton, indigo, etc., etc.

LUCKNOW

is a fine city, and its Immambara and other old royal palatial buildings are well worth a visit, although they lack the solidity of structure which Agra and Delhi can justly boast. They are very pleasing light specimens of oriental modern architecture. Lucknow is a large station, and spoken very highly of by all civil and military officers; it has beautiful parks and charming rides. The country from Lucknow to

CAWNPORE

and Agra is of the same rich agricultural

value which we described above: beautiful to look at, and no doubt yielding most satisfactory returns. Arrived in

AGRA,

we have before us the wonderful monumental structures of the past era of grandeur and magnificence of the "Great Moguls." Description fails and becomes tame in sight of such unparallelled specimens of architecture. They are unique; and anything else in the world, aiming at similar objects, pales by the side of a

"TAJ,"

AND

"ISMUD UL DALLAH,"

OR

"SECUNDRA."

The most fervid imagination of the oriental mind, with its gorgeous and boundless resources, has found expression in these wonderful specimens of Saracenic architecture. The white marble, inlaid with lapis lazuli, malachite, bloodstone, cornelian, agate, and other precious stones, dazzles you in its stupendous masses; the screens, which supply the place of windows in these structures, look at a distance like delicate lace curtains, and, when you come to examine them, you cannot but be astounded at the patience and delicate manipulation which thus transformed the massive blocks of stone into fine lace work. The whole world can show nothing to equal these splendid monuments, and Government have done well to repair the damages which the mutiny and neglect had wrought. The conservative character of the Indian is here again strikingly manifested; the descendants of the original builders of these grand structures are still there, and following the same craft — hence the restoration of the mosaic and inlaid work is followed with religious care and attention by these workmen, and you can scarcely discern the restored from the original. Any description, as we said before, or attempt at description, is in our opinion utterly futile. No pen can convey an adequate notion of the beauty and harmony of the *tout-ensemble.* One must come and see to enjoy these solid relics of ages of gorgeous magnificence, which probably will never return again. From Agra you generally make an excursion to the forsaken city of Akbar,

FUTTEYPORE SIKKRI.

It is only a three hours' drive on a beautiful tamarind-shaded road, and no visitor to Agra should miss it. He will enjoy the novel sensation of sleeping "all alone" in the old palace of Akbar, which has wonderfully well stood its three centuries of desolation, and surrounded by the ruins of the walled town, through which you wind your way for more than half a mile ere you reach the palace. This city and palace were abandoned by Akbar on account, it is said, of the insalubrity of the situation, which is, nevertheless, charming to look at, and probably from some other unknown cause: hence there is no evidence of wilful destruction of anything. The magnificent solid and carved stonework of this palace seeks its equal all over India: it was never surpassed. After you have spent your night and morning in this extraordinary place, and also witnessed the feat of agile divers jumping from the ramparts of the palace, 80 feet high, into the tanks, you take the road to

BHURTPUR,

a railway station, and a typical Indian town, governed still in the old style by an independent rajah: a fine palace beautifully situated; buildings abounding with carved stonework and most quaint picturesque architecture. Hence you take train to

JEYPUR,

likewise the seat of an independent sovereign,

the "Maharajah." The country through which the railway winds is evidently splendid soil, from the produce of cotton and other plants which the cultivated spots carry; but you see everywhere the evidences of slothful government: no order, no cleanliness. This is clearly a vast volcanic region: mounds of rocks and deep ravines everywhere. It is the home of the beautiful mottled sandstone which you see in the monumental structures of Agra, Delhi, etc., and this beautiful material will no doubt find its way further afield when the Trunk Railway, on which we are now travelling, is completed. The fields are overrun with deer, game and peacock, the latter being a holy bird, which no sportsman is allowed to kill. They look very picturesque in droves, but we fear they make great havoc with the seeds of the farmer. Jeypur is a new town: it looks as if it were built to order by a manufacturer of Nürnberg toys; the streets straight, wide, crossing at right angles, where great squares are formed. The town boasts of water and gasworks, and is painted all one colour. The palace is a grand modern structure, where you can see the real life of lazy Orientals; thousands of palace hangers-on crowd the various squares, corridors, verandahs, and apartments. The gardens are most extensive and beautiful. Another novelty we noticed in this palace: although it has some eight or ten stories there was not a single staircase—the roads upwards were all inclined planes, zig-zag or winding in towers, and very easy of ascent. The boudoirs of the harem were wonderful glittering specimens of tawdry imitation of the real grandeur of the old mosaic ornamentation of the Mogul palaces of Agra and Delhi. There is a fine park at Jeypur, and a grand collection of wild animals; the latter seems a favourite amusement of oriental rulers. We had to ride an elephant to view the town and suburbs, as the best mode of taking in all the sights.

A railway to Delhi branches off the main line, and we took this means to reach the latter by a day's journey. We must confess we are here in the same predicament as we were at Agra. The massive, monumental structures of past ages, the enormous extent of the ancient ruins, and the wonderful state of preservation in which they are now found, are beyond our capacity to describe. The pen cannot convey what the eye takes in everywhere, as it roams over the landmarks of ages of civilization which existed at a time when Europe was a howling wilderness. Following these, are spread before you the monuments left by the last Tartar conqueror, the Great Mogul, who is said during his reign to have made this Delhi the great centre of Asiatic trade, when the town's inhabitants were counted by millions, and its revenues were said to amount to £150,000,000 sterling per annum. Such a town one must see: to read about it conveys but a faint glimmer of the reality. You will spend many days here ere you exhaust the multifarious sights of ruins and buildings and sites, which the few meagre guide-books give you; but you may spend weeks profitably if you go roaming among the ancient forts, mosques, palaces, temples, &c., which lie before you at every point of the compass. The fort of New Delhi is probably the most massive and imposing structure of the kind in Asia. It contains the most luxurious palace of the Moguls. Its Dewan-Khas is most gorgeously ornamented, as becomes the site of the once far-famed "Peacock Throne," which was said to be worth £6,000,000 sterling, and was carried off to Persia during one of the numerous raids with which the history of Delhi is teeming. There is no city in the world that has changed hands so often and been the centre of so many conflicts; and as you tread its historical soil you cannot fail to become interested. A view from the Khutoob Minar, a central unique tower, some 240 feet high, lays before you the whole site of ancient and modern Delhi; you can trace the city walls, with a radius of some twelve miles, from this tower, and form an idea of the magnitude of this wonderful "Centre of the World," as it was called in ancient Mogul times.

The trade of the modern Delhi, which yet contains 500,000 inhabitants, is considerable; it is the place of interchange of all the productions of the lowlands with the manufactures of the mountainous regions and tableland of Central Asia. The shawls of Cashmere are marketed here, and the craft of the Delhi goldsmiths is still world-famed. Ladies, especially, will find ample scope to exercise their taste, and their purses, in the great bazaar street, the Chaudney Chauk.

The climate of the whole of this monuniental region, in winter, is simply delicious. The days are warm and sunny, without being oppressive, as the air is dry, crisp and pellucid, and the nights are most pleasantly cool—cold, as the Indians call a temperature of 50° to 60°. We had pleasant wood fires at the hotels always after dinner. You find numerous travellers generally at the hotels—chiefly civilians and military "leaves" in search of health by change from insalubrious stations; and your society, therefore, is generally most intellectual and agreeable, as you have the opportunity of hearing much of all parts of India. I cannot here refrain from paying the "Defenders of the Country" in India the well-deserved compliment, that they are, in India, the most agreeable, pleasant companions, earnest and appreciative of their important duties, free from the absurd, frivolous presumption which, in idle garrison life at home, makes the cloth so unpopular among the industrial classes. They feel in India the weight of their mission; upon their tact and temper depends the safety of the countless millions of peaceful inhabitants; for the great "gros" of the population are men of peace, and will accept any ruler who will leave them undisturbed in their daily avocations. On the other hand there is the turbulent class of the ancient alien conqueror, the Mahomedan Tartar, who is ever ready to take advantage of any commotion that promises plunder, rapine and excitement. These latter it is the province of our battalions to keep in check, and they must therefore remain in the land, in imposing and commanding force, even if there is not a breath of disturbance in the air. The Afghan troubles are looked upon by all military critics whom I have had the advantage of conversing with as a simple outcome of the British situation in India. Peace all over the vast frontier, with a host of lawless, depredatory tribes for neighbours, can never be; but alarm at the ability of our forces to cope with them need never be felt. Exaggeration is a natural sequence, with such elements of gossip, and thus trifling incidents are laid hold of at home for party purposes, and what was a paltry skirmish is dignified by the name of battle. All testimony concurs in the contemptible character of the Afghan forces, and no properly organised body of troops need apprehend disaster by such opponents. The mental enquiry has often occurred to me, when I have watched the habits and ways of the aforesaid Mussulmen, whether there would ever be a time, a sort of millennium, when this hereditary scourge of humanity would disappear. These followers of the Prophet, who preached the religion of hatred in contradistinction of Christ's sublime doctrine of love, seem to be the direct descendants of "Shaitan," as the Hindoos call his infernal majesty. They seem to be born to give trouble to peaceful mankind. Their one end and aim of life seems murder and plunder; work they loathe, their province is to dictate to slaves, whom their plundering raids have made their own. Surely the vengeance of an outraged Deity must descend some time, and clear the most fertile regions of the globe, which they have plundered and desolated, from the Mahomedan scourge. In India we hold them in check, but that is all; convert them to real habits of peace we never shall; and we shall never be able to relax our guard. The expense of these frontier wars is a necessary charge upon the Indian revenue, and it ought always to be borne in sight by the Finance Minister. To talk of exhaustion of resources and inability to bear further taxation is, in my humble opinion, betraying either great ignorance of the country or singular want of enterprise in the financier who propounds such doctrines. In India Government is the owner of the fee simple of the soil, and it is said that the average rental of the whole of this rich country, including all assessed taxation, is below 3s. per acre per annum: this is the so-called land tax which rests on the poor peasant for the use of the land; the only other tax in India which affects him is the salt tax, and that amounts to the insignificant sum of sixpence per head per annum. Hence, we say, talk like the "limit of taxation being arrived at" is nonsense. A country that yielded three centuries ago, when the value of money was tenfold, £150,000,000 to the exchequer is said to be unable to bear a taxation of £50,000,000! Who is to blame for coining such stories, and sending them into circulation until they pass without question? Party government is the culprit; and an amiable desire of the Indian civilian to save his charge from any disagreeable pressure. Well, a bold hand will come some day and firmly assert its right to tax the people, for the people's benefit, and remove the stain of shabby parsimony which taints many government transactions in these days, and brings us into contempt in the eyes of a people who have ever loved to be dazzled by splendid and magnificent dignity.

We have to part from our delightful Delhi at last. Christmas Day is at hand, and we have promised to take our Christmas dinner with some friends in Calcutta. Hence the train direct—a distance of 1,000 miles—is taken, and we land with laudable punctuality on Christmas morn at

CALCUTTA—Howrah Station.

The weather is charming, warmer than Delhi,

but by no means hot. The Great Eastern Hotel is our abode for the next twenty-five days, and although we might expect in a place like Calcutta somewhat more sumptuous entertainment for man and beast in its best caravanserai, it cannot be much grumbled at upon the whole. Its charges are moderate, and that is a considerable recommendation, especially in the eyes of officers with what-mercantile men would consider but scant stipends. The city is most beautifully situated, and its glorious Maidan and Eden-gardens, with the Rotten Row of Calcutta —the Strand—will seek their equal in the world, especially when the wonderfully fine climate of the winter season is put additionally into the balance. The squares and streets are always kept in splendid order, well watered, and, in fact, you might fancy yourself, in December, as being in Paris in Midsummer. Calcutta, in the winter months, is a delightful resort, the temperature ranging from 65° to 75°; the air is balmy and pellucid, and social gaieties abound. Garden parties, dinners, and balls at the palaces and private residences of the opulent inhabitants abound, and strangers are ever hospitably welcomed. It would be invidious to make distinctions where all is measured without stint, but I can't refrain from naming two entertainments at which we had the honour to assist, from their utter novelty most striking to European eyes. One was a ball given by the Maharajah of Hutwah at the Town Hall, to the Viceroy and the Lieutenant-Governor, and to which some 1000 or 1500 of the *élite* of Calcutta society were invited; and the other a "Nautch" in celebration of the wedding of a relative by one of the most opulent citizens of Calcutta, a gentleman named Baboo Durga Churn Law. The former was a most magnificent entertainment in the European style. A grand illumination by many thousand coloured lamps and gas-lights formed a great feature. The crowds of magnificently dressed ladies and natives, in their gorgeous and picturesque dresses, blazing with jewels, was a sight not to be witnessed in Europe. But if this European entertainment was grand, the "Nautch" of Baboo Durga Churn Law was, from its purely Indian character, a sight even better calculated to dazzle European eyes. Here we had the blaze of light in which Orientals delight, both in the illuminated garden and the magnificent reception hall, to welcome a thousand guests, with the native element, in their most gorgeous attire of silks and cloth of gold, studded with jewels, preponderating. An utter absence of ceremony and awkward stiffness, every guest moving freely at pleasure in the crowded rooms, corridors and balconies, with a most sumptuous supply of everything that delights the heart. Gentlemen belonging to the household assiduously distributing bouquets and delicious scents, Indian nautch girls performing in solos and chorus their quaint ceremonial dances; music by bands of richly dressed native musicians, with a full regimental band rendering European music; and everything joyous and merry; refreshments and wines light or substantial, in most sumptuous abundance, suitable to all tastes. Gentlemen at home, who repeat the cant phrase of "the poverty of India," should witness a scene like this, and we warrant they will be cured. This splendid host, a man still in the full prime of life, is the architect of his own great fortune, honestly gained in lawful commerce, and a grand specimen of his race. The expenditure of a lac of rupees upon one entertainment, by a private citizen, does not smack much of the poverty of the country. The Bengal Government, with Sir Ashley Eden, Lieutenant-Governor, is deservedly popular in Calcutta, and you hear only of abundance and content reigning in the Province of Bengal, overflowing exchequer, and great schemes of useful works, which are but waiting the supreme pleasure of "Party Government" at home. There is abundance of money here, and ample resources to back further needs, but the howl at home and the exigencies of the coming election have stopped all progress. The tea districts and the jute country are all badly served with means of modern communication. There are some patches of country, with 600 to the square mile, without a yard of rail, whilst the tea planters are all clamouring for labour. The rail would enable the population from the thick country to transfer itself easily to the thin. All parties interested are most indignant at the delays which have been interposed from home, the reflex of which can't fail to exercise its atom of influence at the coming great party contest. Unfortunately there is no public opinion in India. The European community is too small, and split up too much into cliques. The discipline of the civil service is too severe to allow the clever men to express themselves effectually when they differ from their superiors. Newspapers, although ably conducted, are so cliquish that they fail to lead. The commercial element is too busy—and thus it happens that the whole of the Indian policy discussion is left to "home" professionals and amateurs, many of whom are either wedded to some favourite crotchet, or speak rather from knowledge of the past than of the present. Many argue from information supplied by native outcasts in England, who have no chance of being accurate, as, unfortunately, the absurd Hindoo caste rule makes any native an outcast who leaves his country over sea, and to be an outcast means utter and entire separation from the whole Hindoo community, nearest relatives included. Hence the Government of the country is virtually without any check in the hands of the Civil Service, and it is fortunate that England has such a band of devoted, able men as are to be met with in India. From all accounts, some seasons must be terribly trying to European constitutions, and I have heard of instances of trial and devotion which sound truly heroic: men in charge of districts with delicate young wives, living alone in solitudes without a single European nearer than 100 miles. For services of this kind no remuneration ought to be grudged, and still we hear constant complaints by gentlemen in Parliament of overpaid Indian civilians. We have never met with an exception to the general rule of life for Europeans in India, and that rule is "hard work." With this great responsibility of administration hanging over their heads it cannot be wondered at that the Civil Service look for clear and emphatic declarations of policy always to the "Home Government," and, until such come, they carry out the old lines as suits their convenience and ideas best. "India for the Indians" has been so often and persistently repeated that there is scarcely an atom of regard left for the taxpayer at home. India has to pay her way, they say, that's all. That a conquered country which has cost England hecatombs of lives and treasure should be looked upon as justly due some return to her for the past will never be admitted as long as the note is not changed somewhat and translated thus: "India for the English and Indians." English traders have a right to the protection of their interests as well as Indians have a right to use their own resources upon a fair field and no favour. Mercantile and manufacturing interests in India, especially those conducted by Europeans, are much exercised at the continually widening sphere at which Government operations in manufactures, commerce and agriculture are aiming. Troops of convicts in the numerous gaols must be employed; but it is contended that they should not be employed with the aid of steam and other machinery. Jute mills, oil mills, and print works are all adjuncts of the gaols in India, and can, of course, as they pay no wages, compete most effectually with private enterprise. The ancient leaven of the mercantile character of the Hon. E. I. Company is still very strong in the old C. S., and nothing but the strong hand from Downing Street will reach the cancer. The dignity of the Government of a great empire is compromised by its office-bearers and administrators being ever on the alert to higgle for a bargain in the bazaar. An unmistakable note should be sent forth. The Civil Service are not meant to be clerks and managers of mills, manufacturing establishments, and retail stores or shops. This would conciliate the industrious public, and heal to some extent the breach which exists between mercantile and official circles. We were quite shocked at the general unpopularity which the Government of India (in contradistinction to that of Bengal) at present labours under; it was so different five years ago, when we were here last, and saw Lord Northbrook's rule under the full tide of well-deserved popularity.

We left Calcutta on the 18th January with the British India coasting steamer, which stays a couple of days each at Rangoon, Moulmein and Penang, and thus enables tourists to see the beautiful Burmese country and coast, as well as enjoy the delightful sail upon the calm blue waters of the Bay of Bengal.

RANGOON.

is reached by a long river and difficult navigation between headlands and islands; but you have a charming view of tropical vegetation all along, and we were much impressed with the great capacity for extensive business which spread itself to our view in sailing up the stream. This town is only some twenty-five years old, but already it counts near 100,000 inhabitants. It is regularly laid out, and will eventually become a very handsome place. The trade of this port is increasing at a marvellous ratio; the export of its staple, rice, reaches already some 700,000 tons per annum. Although the idea prevails at home that the interrupted diplomatic relations with King Thebaw of Mandalay would lead to stagnation of trade with Upper Burmah, there is no such result in view at present. The Chinese merchants, who are the chief traders to Upper Burmah, don't concern themselves much with British Burmese politics; they go the even tenor of their ways, and from all accounts, trade through and with Upper Burmah is as flourishing as ever. The steam flotilla, which works the river up to Mandalay, makes its regular trips, and the transit trade to Western China, which is chiefly carried this road, is assuming daily larger proportions. The Burmese are a remarkably pleasant, easy-going people, very different from the Hindoos. They don't meander half their lives away in trifling, gloomy religious observances; they enjoy their days, and spend what they earn, freely. The women hold the purse-strings and are the real "men of business" of the country. They bargain, buying and selling, lending and loaning; in fact, they are like the Parisian ladies of the bourgeoisie, everywhere representatives of the trade of their husbands. They are a race similar to the Japanese, and when we came into their pagodas, which are very extensive, and used chiefly for purposes of feasting, we could have fancied ourselves in Yeddo, so similar is the style of architecture, colour, ornament, and the plan of everything. The great pagodas, which are presided over by Buddha in effigy, as chief intermediary of their communion with the Supreme Being, are all on the tops of hills, in most lovely situations; and here they go, many daily, but most only on holidays, to see and be seen, and amuse themselves, the old ones by intermittent forms of prayer, the young ones by showing their finery.

The political situation need alarm nobody at home: the Burmese are not a martial people. A regiment of British troops would hold Upper Burmah against a dozen Thebaws if our Government were so minded, as the bulk of the people would hail the British as deliverers from distasteful services to their hereditary ruler. However, there seems to be no occasion for action on the part of our Government, and matters will probably be left in *statu quo,* at least such is the general opinion at Rangoon.

The neighbourhood of Rangoon has some charming scenery in lakes and woods, and, as the place is considered very healthy, it should be one of the most pleasant stations in the East. A few years will develope it into a great rival of both Bombay and Calcutta, as far as tonnage is concerned, for, as we stated before, the trade with the vast multitudes of Western China will evidently work itself through this, its natural channel.

MOULMEIN,

our next point, opens out amongst charming

mountain scenery, after we have ascended a long and tortuous river, rather an obstacle to free navigation. Although beautifully situated, this place does not bear the same stamp of coming development and prosperity as Rangoon does so strikingly. The chief trade is in the famous teak timber, and numerous mills are to be seen upon the banks of the river, but, like all other towns the world over, which have been built upon the strength of a wealth of forest at their back, time very shortly arrives when the source of wealth has vanished. Let us hope that the Indian Government, by its forest laws, will arrest the indiscriminate slaughter of these magnificent trees, and make it a condition to replant when the axe is laid at the root of the parent tree. We must not forget to name here the wonderful sight of elephants working at the saw mills and timber yards. The sagacity of the animals is truly astonishing. Their enormous strength is admirably calculated to move and walk off with big tree-logs as if they were walking-sticks. It is complained of generally that there is dearth of labour in Burmah, and both Madras and Chinese coolies earn great wages, hence the elephants are pressed into the service for such ignoble uses. The gaol at Moulmein seemed to be admirably managed: the art of wood carving, which seems to be still in great favour among the Burmese, and of which their pagodas afford fine specimens, is practised at this gaol, and ought to be much encouraged. We were introduced here to a Thug, some Dacoits, and other professional evildoers, who have a task set them at some trade which they are taught or understand, and if they fail to perform this task, the Inspector told us, the infallible remedy was the lash or the cane; this secures steady work.

PENANG,

in the Straits of Malacca, is reached. It has grown very warm here, and you find that the Equator is near. This is a glorious tropical landscape, as fine as Ceylon: the harbour is filled with craft of all sorts; you see plainly a new region is before you; the Chinese junks and the Malay trading craft prevail here, with the long-tailed gentry predominating. Splendid estates are here owned by an English firm, and yield princely incomes. Pepper, nutmeg and cocoa-nuts are the chief staples of this port; they are brought, for shipment to Europe, from all the surrounding islands, and Penang is on the high tide of prosperity. Another thirty hours brings us to

SINGAPORE.

The latitude is 1° 40′ N. and the temperature 90° in the shade, but this is soon reduced by mighty showers of rain, which convert the streets in a few minutes into rapid water-courses. The climate is generally temperate, an average of 76° to 78° the year round, and Singapore bears the character of a very healthy place. It has a lovely bay, and the suburbs are delightfully situated in groves of glorious palms and other tropical vegetation.

The place bears the stamp of great prosperity and is evidently bound to become the Liverpool of the East, as it is the convenient depôt and mart of interchange between Orient and Occident. The products of all the islands and adjacent Malay mainland find their market here, whilst on the other hand Chinamen, Bornese, Javanese, and all the numerous races of this populous region come here to supply the wants tendered them by civilization. It is a most interesting, pleasant place to spend a few days, as you see every nation and race from the face of the globe represented here. The bay always boasts of men-of-war of some nation, and the European inhabitants don't seem to be so anxious to exchange their pleasant tropical quarters as Anglo-Indians elsewhere generally are. This was the terminal point of our winter tour, and we transferred ourselves on board the passing China mail steamer for Galle and Suez on the 4th February. It happened, by singular coincidence, that we met the same P. & O. which brought us out, and our trip was therefore made doubly pleasant from meeting old friends. The voyage along the Straits and across the blue waters of the Indian Ocean is most enjoyable, albeit the temperature keeps all along to 85° upwards. We are going on the same parallel, and this is the region of tropical thunderstorms, which are far from unpleasant. The lightning, which illuminates the heavens all night long, is a glorious phenomenon. The rest of our journey is of the usual pleasant character, and we are now welcoming Old England, after an absence of nearly five months, with feelings of unmixed delight at having escaped the severe winter. We have spent a most pleasant time throughout, and cannot but wonder that more winter tours are not laid in the same direction. The travelling is easy and luxurious, the hotels fairly good, the feeding excellent, the climate delicious, and society everywhere irreproachable and English. The sights in every respect are novel, and, for our part, we think them infinitely better worth investigating than Ancient Rome, Greece, or even Egypt.

APPENDIX.

Report issued to the Salt Chamber of Commerce, Northwich, April, 1880.

SALT IN INDIA.

(No. 2.)

NOTES OF A TOUR, 1879-80.

THE equalization of the salt duties which took place last year has resulted in unmitigated success, and ought to encourage Indian financiers to deal with other fiscal matters, upon equally broad sound grounds, without being scared by the ancient timid axioms, that the Indian revenue is inelastic, and that the country is poverty stricken. The salt revenue might be made the most convenient and just medium by which the necessities of the State could be met. The taxpayer barely feels any slight alteration in the salt duties, revenue is obtained without direct oppressive intervention of the salt collector, the paltry trifle of sixpence per annum, which is the real sum total per head of the present salt duty, divided by 365 daily payments of each taxpayer, (for salt is bought in the bazaar only for daily consumption by the masses), is never felt, even if it were added to. But Government should give up its odious, ostentatious monopoly dealings, and collect the tax, as it does in Calcutta, indirectly, at the customhouse. The thousands of officials, who are now looked upon as so many tax collectors, and the hundreds of thousands of coolies, eking out a miserable existence by manufacturing an inferior article, should disappear as they have done in Bengal, and not offend the taxpayer by flaunting their occupation in his face. The salt revenue will yield this year probably upwards of seven millions sterling at the equalization rate of 2rs. 8a. per maund, hence every 4a. would give 700,000 pounds sterling, and if the finances require a few millions extra, a single stroke of the pen would give the amount to the exchequer, without really adding any appreciable burthen to the taxpayer.

At *Bombay* I was informed that the rise of the duty, viz., from the 1r. 13a. to the equalization rate of 2rs. 8a. per maund had been simply productive of a large increase of revenue without affecting consumption in the least. Government had acquired by bargain with the Portuguese the salt works at Goa, which were giving them considerable trouble for a long time, as they supplied the smuggling trade all along the coast. It is to be hoped that Government will terminate the manufacture in this region, as it can never pay, or contribute to the dignity of British Government to extend monopoly manufacture over foreign territory. There is already sadly too much of this old heritage of the "Hon. E. I. Company" in British Indian territory.

In the *North-West Provinces*, which are now united

under one salt district with the Central Provinces and the Punjaub, there is an enormous increase of quantity consumed, since the equalization of the duties, and although the duty has been reduced from 3rs. to 2rs. 8a. per maund the revenue shows vast increase.

To some extent this increase is to be accounted for by a new treaty with the independent States of Rajpootana, in result of the abolition of the salt line, and which brings the hitherto untaxed subjects of the Rajpoot States under the thumb of the British tax collector. However, the chief cause of the vast increase of the Sambuhr lake revenue lies, in my opinion, in the fact, that this salt is most unduly favoured in the matter of duty, as against its English competitor. Before the equalization the difference between the tax in the North West and Bengal (which is supplied chiefly by English salt) was 4a. per maund, in order to allow the salt from the Punjaub mines a chance to meet the salt from the South. When this arrangement was made, Sambuhr salt was not considered, as it belonged to a foreign State, and did not much interfere with British produce. The equalization was determined on, the Sambuhr lake leased by Government, and since then it has become the great source of salt supply for the whole of the Central District. And I presume, in order to show a good face on the revenue accounts, the last budget increased the difference of duty between the North-West and Bengal Districts, or in other words between Sambuhr and English salt to 6a. per maund, *i. e., a pound sterling per ton in favour of Sambuhr to the detriment of English salt.* The harmony of the whole scheme has also suffered to that extent, inasmuch as the largest province of the Empire—Bengal—has been denied the full advantage of the equalization—the duty having been reduced not to the equalization rate of 2rs. 8a. but to 2rs. 14a. only, with a promise that the real levelling should follow. Sambuhr therefore is flourishing, as well it may do with a *protective duty of £1 per ton*, and English salt is made to hold its own with difficulty in all the districts where the two meet, and solely through its superior quality. It was formerly stated that the people who were supplied by Sambuhr salt liked its dirty blue and red colour (the result of mixture of mud in the brine), but it seems that this taste is dying out, as the report of the department states that the white salt which is got in some parts of the lake now is much preferred. It is a wholesome sign of the times that Government officials will at last admit that pure white salt is really the article most desired and desirable for consumption.

The anomaly of this differential duty, it is hoped, will be cured this Budget.* I have remonstrated on the subject at Calcutta, and met at head-quarters

---

* Since the above was written the Budget is out, but makes no alteration,—it simply deals in an empty promise without a definite date.

with every consideration. The letter I append was addressed by me to the Government of India at the instance of an honourable member of Council. I hope it will have the desired effect. Since the equalization scheme has been carried out, the excise manufacture in the neighbourhood of Calcutta has also shown signs of fresh life. The reason is apparent. Notwithstanding the bargain which the Salt Chamber made originally with the Indian Home Government under Sir Charles Wood, the excise-made article has again been granted a differential protective duty. Whilst Liverpool salt pays 2rs. 14a. Pooree only pays 2rs. 8a. In addition to this highly protective figure of £1 per ton; considerable privileges have been further granted to the manufacturers in freeing them from the cost of police supervision, which they formerly had to pay. The result is of course a considerably increased native manufacture. The administration report gives excise manufacture—

1877-8—1,70,986 maunds,

1878-9—5,84,394 „

an increase of 241 per cent, or about 16,000 tons. Along with this increase, of which the district officers are justly proud, as it proves their zeal,—the ugly feature of the case is, from a broader point of view, that this paltry make of about 22,000 tons per annum necessitated 1,437 prosecutions in the criminal courts, whereas the whole Calcutta offences against the salt laws, viz., the Howrah cases, which deal with about 280,000 tons, comprise only 15 prosecutions. The self-evident conclusion of these facts is, that this manufacture is liable to considerable illicit dealings in the article. I therefore ask: is it sound policy for the Government to protect and hold out great inducements to such a trade, in order to damage legitimate commerce in English salt?

The aforenamed causes have naturally contributed to deprive the import of sea-borne salt of its proper development. The figures have remained almost stationary, although the pure quality of the English salt is gaining more favour, and where not unduly weighted with differential prices, is taking wider range. I do not for a moment blame the subaltern officers, who administer the salt department and manufacture of Government salt, both in the case of Sambuhr and Excise salt, as it is but natural that they should endeavour to widen the range and protect their salt against English imports; which, from their point of view, is an interloper and competitor. But the supreme Government has to take a wider circle of judgment, both the fiscal and the commercial policy are involved, and the mercantile interests have a right to demand fair play. It is likewise the duty of Government not to force the people indirectly to consume an inferior article as food. The vicious taste of the people in the districts which afford saltpetre grounds is manifested and encouraged by the inferior salt they are made to consume from the monopoly manufacture. The Madras report teems with complaints of illicit consumption of so-called "earth-salts." These are chiefly noxious bittern salts gathered in places where saltpetre is made, a result in the latter manufacture, and from the manure heaps of the villagers, where the ground has become so saturated with the urine and droppings from the cattle and their masters, that, in the hot Indian climate, saltpetre is produced by the simple action of sun and air. Common salt likewise results in these combinations; and this stuff, called "earth salt," the people eat, because they consider it as good as the Government monopoly salt. I have nothing to say against the chemical constitution of the Sambuhr salt, although it is dirty and mud-mixed, and cannot compare with English salt; but I say again, as I have said before, the sea salt on the Bay of Bengal coast is a simple abomination, and it is unworthy the name of a wholesome article of food, *issued with the stamp of the British Empire*, which still clings tenaciously to the monopoly manufacture in Madras. I am fully aware that it is of little use repeating the old arguments—Commissions have sat and cavilled with details, and may sit again and recommend; but they will alter nothing. A strong hand alone, *at Downing Street*, will produce the salutary effect, and we shall have to wait for another Sir Charles Wood, who dictated the despatch which sent the similar pet manufacture of Bengal to sleep, with a result upon which everybody congratulates the people and the administration. The same arguments were current then, in opposition, as you find now in the mouths of the defenders of the Madras monopoly. It was then said the people will rather eat the dirt made at their own door, than the pure white salt brought to them over the sea. Let them go to Calcutta to-day, and they will see that the market value of each cargo is appreciated by the nicest comparisons of shades of white.

A few facts and figures which I have taken from the last administration report of the *Madras Salt Department* will speak for themselves; they require no comment.

The monopoly manufacture, which is in round numbers nearly equal to the sea-borne salt trade of Calcutta—about 250,000 tons—employs in Madras 2,787 police—prosecuted last year 9,563, and convicted 8,252 persons, for illicit dealings in salt. In Calcutta the number of cases was 15, as I stated above. The analysis of the produce in 1876 showed au average of but 84·82 per cent. chloride of sodium or common salt, organic matter 1·88. Chloride of magnesium and other foreign salt, 4·12; moisture 9·18—100. At two important stations the chloride of sodium was as low as 74·6 at Neidavagal, and 77·8 at Negapatam.

Any return of the real net revenue derived from salt in Madras, as compared with that for an equal quantity obtained from Bengal, of sea-borne salt, would be very instructive.

There is a general call for Madras coolies all over the East; Burmah, Assam, Bengal, all are short of labour, and the former excuse, that the salt manufacture gives bread to a great number, won't apply now. The salt mauufacture pays starvation wages, compared to what men earn in the above district as labourers.

I am happy to report of Burmah that English salt is gradually and firmly asserting itself, both for the consumption of British as well as Upper Burmah and the districts adjoining, belonging to China and the Shans. There is now a very extensive transit trade, growing, with rapid strides, through Rangoon *via* Mandalay, with the caravan routes of Western China. Chinamen will buy entire cargoes of salt for transport up the Rangoon river, *via* Mandalay. The duty is only one per cent. *ad val.* for transit, whilst for consumption in British Burmah it is 3a. per maund. From all I have heard on the spot, and the investigations I made, I should consider any alteration of these figures at present hazardous; it might destroy the growing trade with China. The native manufacture of Burmah, although still at a considerable figure—16,000 tons—is evidently doomed to die at an early date, before the advancing lights of purity of the imported salts. Their mode of manufacture is very elaborate, in small earthen pots stacked like a bee-hive, and fired with junglewood. The produce, like all salt produced from the water of the Bay of Bengal, is dirty and impure.

The Straits Settlements, Penang, and Singapore, are both considerable importers of salt for manuring the cocoa-nut tree, which, it seems, cannot flourish without salt. They take 6,000 to 7,000 tons annually each, and have their wants supplied partly from the French manufacture at Saigon, and occasionally also from Ceylon, which is likewise a *British Colony monopoly manufacture.* Private trade can't of course succeed in lines of traffic where Government chooses to compete, and under one name or another gives advantages which the individual can't afford to contend against. It will, however, be well for the salt trade of England to keep its eye on these places, as they are growing markets, and Government some day or other, whether Indian or Colonial, will possibly return from its monopoly predilections.

Salt Chamber of Commerce of Northwich,
Dated Calcutta, 8th January, 1880.

R. B. Chapman, Esq., Secretary to the Government of India,
Financial Department.

SIR,—I take the opportunity of my presence in India to draw the attention of Government to the urgent desirability which exists for carrying out the settled policy of equalization of the Salt Duties, to its final and complete conclusion.

The Government is aware that this Chamber has for ten years advocated the measure, and they cannot but frankly acknowledge that their views have been concurrent with the Government measure of last Budget, and they have therefore accepted without remonstrance, as a temporary measure, which the immediate future would rectify, the disadvantage at which sea imports were placed.

However, the interests of the English Salt Trade are beginning to suffer seriously, and the Chamber cannot, consistently with the interests which it guards, refrain from urgent pressure upon the Government to take the next step in the forthcoming Budget, and reduce, as far as financial considerations will permit, the Bengal higher duty on sea imported salt. *English salt simply asks for fair play*, and it is not just, after the experience of the past 30 years, to handicap it again, in favour of the native produce to the *extent of nearly a pound sterling per ton.*

I hope the Government will give due consideration to my respectful remonstrances and apply the remedy.

I have the honour to subscribe myself,

Your obedient humble servant,

H. E. FALK.